SPECIAL DAYS

NATIONAL SORRY DAY

JANE PFEIFFER

Redback Publishing
Suite 6, 13a Narabang Way,
Belrose NSW 2085
Australia

www.redbackpublishing.com
orders@redbackpublishing.com

ISBN 978-1-761401-60-2

Author: Jane Pfeiffer
Editor: Caroline Thomas
Design: Redback Publishing

Acknowledgements
Abbreviations: l—left, r—right, b—bottom, t—top, c—centre, m—middle
We would like to thank the following for permission to reproduce photographs: (Images © shutterstock, wikimedia commons)

p6 Philip Schubert / Shutterstock,
p7 ChameleonsEye/Shutterstock,
p11t Orion Media Group / Shutterstock,
p11b Islandjems - Jemma Craig / Shutterstock,
p12-13 Serge Goujon / Shutterstock,
p13t Australian Human Rights Commission, CC BY 2.0 via Wikimedia Commons,
p13b Philip Schubert / Shutterstock,
p14 Holli / Shutterstock,
p19t State Library of South Australia / SLSA reference D 7546(Misc),
p20t PomInOz / Shutterstock.com,
p21t PomInOz / Shutterstock.com,
21b ChameleonsEye / Shutterstock,
p22t Tom Jastram / Shutterstock,
p22 Walk for Reconciliation / Image courtesy of photographer: C.Moore Hardy, City of Sydney Archives, A-00069112,
p23 Mari Nelson / Shutterstock,
p24t PomInOz / Shutterstock,
p25 LittlePanda29 / Shutterstock,
p28-29 Philip Schubert / Shutterstock

NATIONAL LIBRARY OF AUSTRALIA
A catalogue record for this book is available from the National Library of Australia

CONTENTS

The author and publisher acknowledge the Traditional Owners of this land and recognise their continuing connection to Country. We pay our respects to Aboriginal and Torres Strait Islander cultures and to Elders past, present and emerging. Aboriginal and Torres Strait Islander peoples should be aware that this book may contain images or names of people who have since passed away.

SPECIAL DAYS

In Australia we celebrate or commemorate a number of special days throughout the year. Some are public holidays, which means that people can have the day off work or school. Some special days are marked with events and festivities.

Many special days in Australia commemorate something of historical importance. This gives Australians the opportunity to recognise how people and events have shaped our Nation. Australia is a multicultural society with a federation of states and territories. Some special days are significant only to a particular state. Some are important to a specific culture, community or religious group.

Australia is a federation of states and territories, so some special days are significant only to a particular state.

Australia Day

LEST WE FORGET

Anzac Day

National Sorry Day

Clean Up Australia Day

Melbourne Cup Day

The King's Birthday

Special days are a chance to reflect on the past, to appreciate the world we know and to look to the future together. On these days, we celebrate some of the things that make Australia what it is today.

NATIONAL SORRY DAY

Soon after European colonialists began to settle in Australia in the late 1700s, Aboriginal children began to be taken from their families. These wrongdoings were a misguided attempt to protect the children from their existing ways of living. The European settlers did not yet understand or appreciate the Indigenous peoples' cultures, customs, spiritual beliefs or custodianship of the land. The act of removing Indigenous children from their families continued until the 1970s.

National Sorry Day is a time to reflect on how these wrongdoings have affected and continue to affect Australia's Aboriginal and Torres Strait Islander peoples and their cultures. It is also a time to consider what reconciliation means for the future of all Australians.

DAY: National Sorry Day
DATE: 26 May
WHERE: All states and territories
WHAT: An annual event to recognise and apologise for the mistreatment of Aboriginal and Torres Strait Islander peoples, particularly in respect to the Stolen Generations

A LONG HISTORY

Aboriginal and Torres Strait Islander peoples have lived on the land that we now call Australia for over 60,000 years. However, since the colonisation of Australia that began in 1788, Australia's Indigenous peoples have been severely mistreated.

Aboriginal and Torres Strait Islander peoples have been the custodians of Australia since the Dreaming. For tens of thousands of years, they have respectfully cared for its plants, animals and water supplies, and have nurtured the spiritual connections between all things. Australia's First Peoples defined countries within Australia, each with their own languages, beliefs and laws, and they enjoyed well-established trading relationships for goods such as tools, medicines and weapons, as well as stories, music and art.

Foreign settlement was a tragic experience for the Indigenous people. They suffered great hardship through violence and disease in a way that they had never experienced before. They were unable to defend against these new threats, resulting in their lands and traditional ways of life being taken from them.

THE STOLEN GENERATIONS

Some of Australia's darkest times include the years of the Stolen Generations. During these times, thousands of Aboriginal children were taken away from their families and placed in orphanages so that European culture could be imposed on them.

After decades of forced removals, the Australian government decided to impose a policy of assimilation, in a bid to make all of the people who lived in Australia hold the same beliefs and behave in the same way. This policy was enforced between 1951 and 1962, and caused many thousands more Aboriginal and Torres Strait Islander children to be actively sought out and forcibly removed from their families. Even after the Assimilation Policy ended, Indigenous children continued to be forcibly removed into the mid 1970s.

Life for these children was extremely difficult. Many suffered abuse from those who were supposed to care for them, while others were forced into slavery.

Often, the children were denied essentials such as food and new clothing, and very few received a level of education that might lead to well-paid and independent work roles in their new communities. They became known as the Stolen Generations.

ASSIMILATION

Despite its ill-informed intentions and harmful effects, Australia's Assimilation Policy in regard to First Nations peoples forced their plight before the eyes of the general public. Most non-Indigenous people had never before witnessed the results of the forced separations of Indigenous children, and the hurt this caused to them, their families and their communities.

Before the policy took effect, Aboriginal and Torres Strait Islander peoples were treated according to very misguided beliefs. Their cultures, traditions and ways of life were completely misunderstood and feared by the new settlers, who had very different cultural practices.

Many children were taken from their families due to the wrong belief that they were being 'rescued'. The Assimilation Policy made these misguided acts of discrimination and persecution legal. With approval and power from the Government, non-Indigenous Australians were actively encouraged and employed to enforce the removal of Indigenous culture from Australia.

The Assimilation Policy forced both Indigenous and other Australians to face the almost 200-year-old problem of assimilation and its disastrous outcomes. Tensions overflowed and Indigenous voices finally began to be heard.

The Assimilation Policy brought cultural differences charging into the spotlight and, in the process, drew the Indigenous peoples' suffering into the spotlight too.

Many people began to question the policy and the treatment of Aboriginal and Torres Strait Islander peoples. Over time, these efforts reached the attention of the Government.

THE REFERENDUM

In 1967, five years after the Government scrapped the Assimilation Policy, non-Indigenous Australians voted in a referendum at which they were asked the question:

Do you approve the proposed law for the alteration of the Constitution entitled 'An Act to alter the Constitution so as to omit certain words relating to the people of the Aboriginal race in any state so that Aboriginals are to be counted in reckoning the population'?

Almost 94 percent of the non-Indigenous population voted and over 90 percent of those people voted 'Yes'. They wanted Aboriginal and Torres Strait Islander peoples to have the same rights as other Australians and were beginning to understand that their treatment of Indigenous peoples and their cultures had been very misguided.

Over the next two decades since the referendum of 1967, both non-Indigenous and Indigenous Australians worked hard to explain the problems facing Aboriginal and Torres Strait Islander peoples to the Government and to suggest solutions. However, progress was then and still remains slow.

Australia is yet to develop a formal treaty between the government and the Indigenous peoples who lived on the land before Europeans arrived. There are many issues that continue to be disputed, including land rights and ownership, culturally appropriate laws, environmentally sensitive practices and the sacred status of many things and places.

Many areas of Indigenous culture are still mysterious to most non-Indigenous Australians. Large parts of this culture became lost and it will take much work and reconciliation before it can be better understood by all, and appropriately managed and preserved by Aboriginal and Torres Strait Islander peoples.

THE RECONCILIATION COUNCIL

Many people have attempted to resolve the issues that surround Indigenous relations in Australia and these actions led to the Council for Aboriginal Reconciliation being established in 1991. It had 25 members, including 12 Aboriginal people and two Torres Strait Islanders. The Council's aim was to discuss, create and exchange commitments for reconciliation in the lead up to the one-hundredth anniversary of Federation in 2001. By 1997, the Australian Government was ready to hold an investigation into the policy of forced removal of Aboriginal and Torres Strait Islander children from their families.

PROF. TOM CALMA, AO, CO-CHAIR OF RECONCILIATION AUSTRALIA, 2022

Government representatives listened to hundreds of Aboriginal and Torres Strait Islander accounts of being taken, or of having their children taken away from families and communities. The report showed a deep need for an official acknowledgement and apology for the enormous suffering of those Stolen Generations and their loved ones who were left behind.

The final report was called: *The National Inquiry into the Separation of Aboriginal and Torres Strait Islander Children from their Families*. Thereafter known as *Bringing Them Home*, this critical report paved the way for the very first National Sorry Day on 26 May, 1998.

MOLLY'S STORY

MOLLY KELLY (CRAIG)

Molly was a descendant of the Mardudjara people. She was born in 1915 at Jigalong in the east Pilbara. In 1931, Molly, her sister Daisy and their cousin Gracie were taken away from their families and sent to the Moore River Mission. The day after they arrived, the girls escaped and started the long walk home. It took them nine weeks to walk 1,600 kilometres. Molly found her way home by following the rabbit-proof fence.

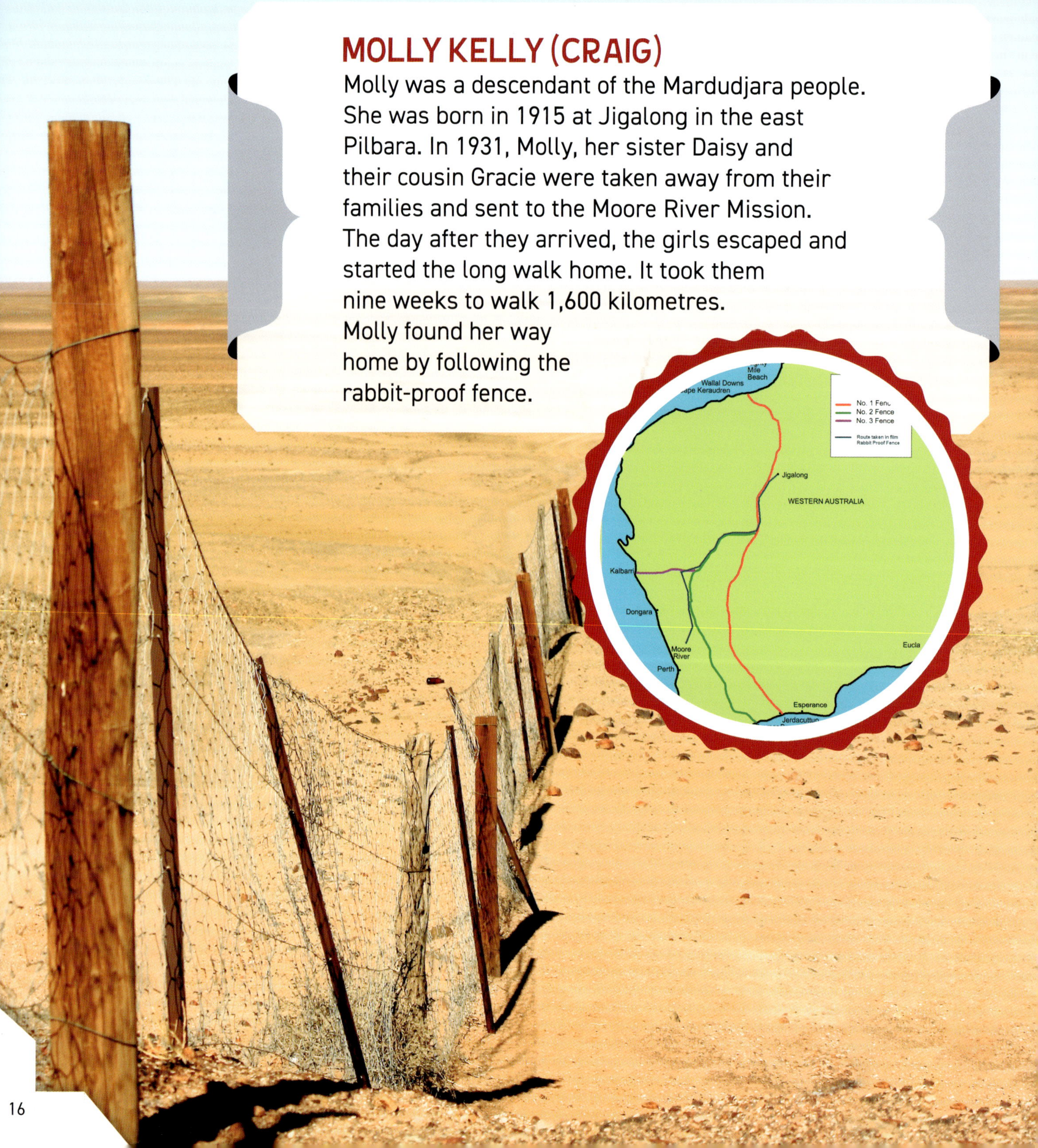

Molly was taken to Moore River again in 1940 with her two young daughters. Once more, she ran away taking her younger daughter with her but leaving her older daughter, Doris, behind. Molly didn't see Doris again for 21 years.

Doris wrote a book about her mother's journey called *Follow the Rabbit-Proof Fence*. It was later made into a movie.

THE SORRY BOOKS

After the 1997 *Bringing Them Home* report, one thousand Sorry Books were created and signed by about half a million people.

Most Sorry Books are now held by local Indigenous Communities. The Australian Institute of Aboriginal and Torres Strait Islander Studies (AIATSIS) in Canberra now holds over 500 Sorry Books.

Each Sorry Book begins with the following statement:

By signing my name in this book, I record my deep regret for the injustices suffered by Indigenous Australians as a result of European settlement and, in particular, I offer my personal apology for the hurt and harm caused by the forced removal of children from their families and for the effect of government policy on the human dignity and spirit of Indigenous Australians.

I would also like to record my desire for reconciliation and for a better future for all our peoples. I make a commitment to a united Australia, which respects this land of ours, values Aboriginal and Torres Strait Islander heritage, and provides justice and equity for all.

The remaining pages are filled with signatures and comments to represent a people's apology. Australians added their names in different ways. Some wrote longer apologies. Others simply signed their names. Many children drew images that symbolised the event for them. The books were displayed all over the country, at schools, in churches and in community halls.

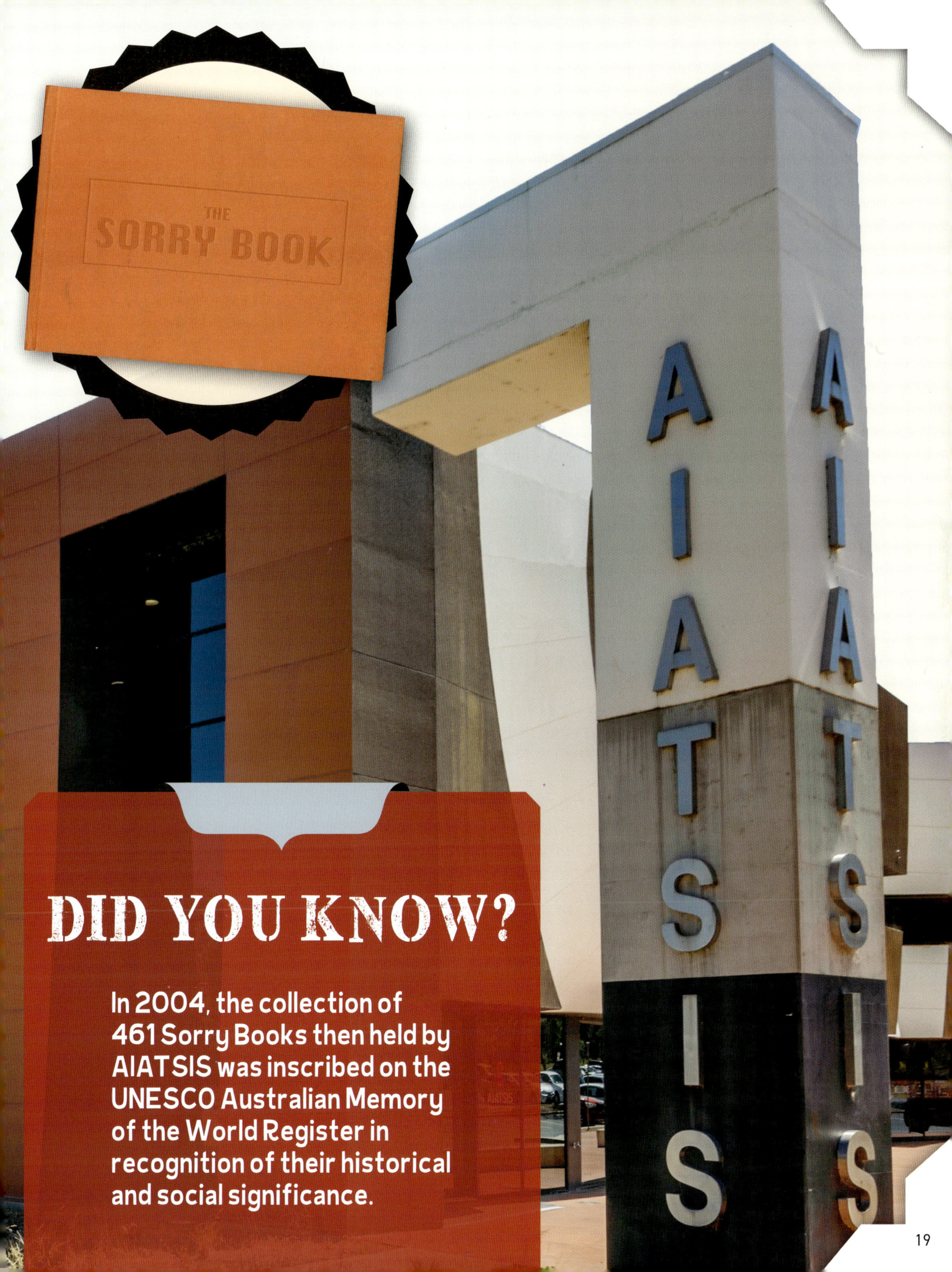

DID YOU KNOW?

In 2004, the collection of 461 Sorry Books then held by AIATSIS was inscribed on the UNESCO Australian Memory of the World Register in recognition of their historical and social significance.

NATIONAL SORRY DAYS

On 26 May, 1998, Australia held its first National Sorry Day. Hundreds of thousands of Australians took part in events all around Australia, writing in Sorry Books and apologising to Indigenous people for the suffering caused to their families and communities.

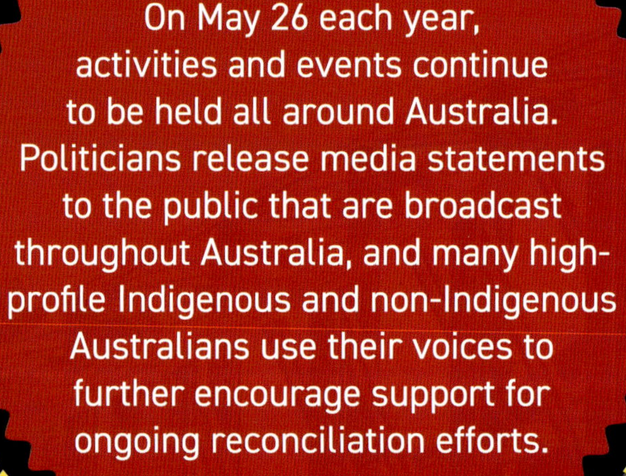

On May 26 each year, activities and events continue to be held all around Australia. Politicians release media statements to the public that are broadcast throughout Australia, and many high-profile Indigenous and non-Indigenous Australians use their voices to further encourage support for ongoing reconciliation efforts.

National Sorry Day is a time for all Australians to learn about the history of Australia's First Peoples, the Stolen Generations and what reconciliation means.

National Sorry Day became a way for Australians to apologise to Aboriginal and Torres Strait Islander people for their suffering and, in particular, the suffering of children, parents and the communities of the Stolen Generations. National Sorry Day is an important part of the reconciliation process because it acknowledges the pain that was caused by removing Aboriginal and Torres Strait Islander children from their families.

A WALK FOR RECONCILIATION

Corroboree 2000 was held on 27 May, 2000 at the Sydney Opera House, in readiness for the one-hundredth anniversary of Australian Federation in 1901.

National Sorry Day 2000 included a march across the Sydney Harbour Bridge. It was the largest number of people to have ever marched for a cause in Australia. More than 250,000 Australians took part as a way of saying sorry to the Stolen Generations and to show their support for reconciliation between Indigenous and non-Indigenous peoples. Elsewhere in Australia, over 100,000 more people marched for reconciliation.

A NEW REFERENDUM

In 2017, at the First Nations National Constitutional Convention at Uluru, council member Megan Davis delivered the Uluru Statement from the Heart. This was developed by a 16-member Referendum Council of Indigenous and non-Indigenous community leaders, with the aim of delivering constitutional recognition of the rights of Aboriginal and Torres Strait Islander peoples. Fifty years on from the referendum that gave Indigenous Australians the constitutional right to be counted as Australians, Aboriginal and Torres Strait Islander peoples were still waiting for formal recognition in Australia's Constitution.

AN OPPORTUNITY TO LEARN

Australia has a rich history, with two sides to our national story. National Sorry Day is now included as an important part of the Australian school curriculum so that new generations of Australians can better understand and appreciate reconciliation.

Many schools take part in National Sorry Day activities during NAIDOC week to learn about the Stolen Generations. Activities include writing stories and essays, and lighting candles for those Indigenous Australians who were taken. Local Indigenous Elders visit schools to speak with students and some schools show and discuss movies that focus on the Stolen Generations.

INTO THE FUTURE

National Sorry Day is now an important part of the Australian events calendar. All across the country, millions of Australians now take part in events on this special day. People attend morning teas, lunches and concerts. Aboriginal artists perform, and community leaders and Indigenous Australian Elders and educators make speeches and answer questions. There are Aboriginal and Torres Strait Islander flag raising events, as well as walks and marches for reconciliation.

SMOKING CEREMONY

Many Indigenous people attend smoking ceremonies at corroborees. These are very special events that bring the present day into line with the Dreaming time, using sacred song, dance and art to celebrate all of Creation. As part of National Sorry Day, non-Indigenous Australians are invited to attend to learn more about Indigenous cultures, beliefs and spiritual connections to the land we call Australia.

We now know how the impact of European colonisation and the policies and laws that followed had a devastating impact on the lives of Indigenous Australians.
It is critical that all Australians work together to support Aboriginal and Torres Strait Islander peoples to reclaim, rebuild and preserve their culture into the future. In north and central Australia, some aspects of traditional life have survived and even thrived, and there is now emerging hope for the revival of Indigenous cultural awareness across Australia's cities and suburbs.

THE IMPORTANCE OF COMMUNITY ELDERS MAKING DECISIONS

Community Elders make decisions for their community based on their deep knowledge of traditional law, ceremony and language. It is very important that this knowledge is actively lived and learned by the young and taught by their Elders. This connection to culture was taken away from the Stolen Generations, but is now acknowledged as essential for Indigenous people to heal and move forward.

BEING RAISED AT HOME

It is critical that Aboriginal and Torres Strait Islander children engage in traditional activities and learn their local Aboriginal and Torres Strait Islander languages and cultural practices, while participating in other schooling activities. In this way, Aboriginal Australians and Torres Strait Islander peoples will have the opportunity to heal so that true reconciliation can evolve.

SAYING SORRY

On 27 May, 1997, the Western Australian Government was the first state government to issue an apology to Australia's Aboriginal and Torres Strait Islander people. By 2001, all state and territory governments had issued apologies. The Federal Government, under Prime Minister John Howard at the time, declined to do this.

Opposition leader, Kevin Rudd, supported making a formal public apology to the victims of the Stolen Generations. In 2007, the Labor Party won the federal election and The Apology was the first item of business when Parliament opened in 2008.

On 13 February, 2008, the Australian Government's Apology to Australia's Indigenous peoples was witnessed by thousands of people gathered in Canberra and was broadcast live on television around the Nation. This formal apology to Indigenous Australians for forced removals of Australian Indigenous children from their families by Australian federal and state government agencies was seen by many as a huge step forward towards reconciliation.

Apology to Australia's Indigenous Peoples

House of Representatives
Parliament House, Canberra

The Speaker of the House (Hon Harry Jenkins MP): The Clerk.

The Clerk: Government business notice number 1, Motion offering an apology to Australia's Indigenous peoples.

The Speaker: Prime Minister.

Prime Minister (Hon Kevin Rudd MP): Mr Speaker, I move:

That today we honour the Indigenous peoples of this land, the oldest continuing cultures in human history.

We reflect on their past mistreatment.

We reflect in particular on the mistreatment of those who were Stolen Generations – this blemished chapter in our nation's history.

The time has now come for the nation to turn a new page in Australia's history by righting the wrongs of the past and so moving forward with confidence to the future.

We apologise for the laws and policies of successive Parliaments and governments that have inflicted profound grief, suffering and loss on these our fellow Australians.

We apologise especially for the removal of Aboriginal and Torres Strait Islander children from their families, their communities and their country.

For the pain, suffering and hurt of these Stolen Generations, their descendants and for their families left behind, we say sorry.

To the mothers and the fathers, the brothers and the sisters, for the breaking up of families and communities, we say sorry.

And for the indignity and degradation thus inflicted on a proud people and a proud culture, we say sorry.

We the Parliament of Australia respectfully request that this apology be received in the spirit in which it is offered as part of the healing of the nation.

For the future we take heart; resolving that this new page in the history of our great continent can now be written.

We today take this first step by acknowledging the past and laying claim to a future that embraces all Australians.

A future where this Parliament resolves that the injustices of the past must never, never happen again.

A future where we harness the determination of all Australians, Indigenous and non-Indigenous, to close the gap that lies between us in life expectancy, educational achievement and economic opportunity.

A future where we embrace the possibility of new solutions to enduring problems where old approaches have failed.

A future based on mutual respect, mutual resolve and mutual responsibility.

A future where all Australians, whatever their origins, are truly equal partners, with equal opportunities and with an equal stake in shaping the next chapter in the history of this great country, Australia.

The Hon Kevin Rudd MP
Prime Minister
February 13th, 2008

THE ABORIGINAL FLAG AND THE TORRES STRAIT ISLANDER FLAG

Australia has three official flags: the Australian National Flag, the Australian Aboriginal Flag and the Torres Strait Islander Flag. In 2022, the Australian Aboriginal Flag replaced the flag of New South Wales, to fly permanently alongside the Australian National Flag atop the Sydney Harbour Bridge. This change is an important step towards healing and reconciliation.

THE AUSTRALIAN ABORIGINAL FLAG

The Australian Aboriginal Flag was first flown on National Aborigines Day in July 1971 and became the official flag for the Aboriginal Tent Embassy in Canberra in 1972. It was declared one of Australia's national flags in July 1995. In 2022, the Australian Government bought the copyright to the flag design from artist Harold Thomas, so that anyone can now freely reproduce and use the design.

Black represents the Aboriginal people
Yellow circle represents the Sun
Red (ochre) represents the earth

THE TORRES STRAIT ISLANDER FLAG

The Torres Strait Islander Flag was designed by Bernard Namok and was first used in May 1992 at the Torres Strait Cultural Festival. It was declared one of Australia's national flags in July 1995.

Blue represents the sea
Green represents the land
Two black stripes represent the people
White Dhari is a traditional headdress
Five-pointed white star symbolises the five island groups and the navigational importance of stars to the seafaring peoples of the Torres Strait

GLOSSARY

apology recognising wrongdoings, feeling bad about them and taking action to correct the harm caused

assimilation belief that all people should behave according to the same culture, spiritual beliefs, laws and moral codes

colonisation settlement in a foreign land and imposing foreign culture and law upon it

commemorate to honour the memory of something or someone with a ceremony or celebration

constitutional according to the set of principles that are used by government

corroboree Australian Aboriginal ceremony in the form of sacred rituals or informal gatherings

custodians people who have responsibility for taking care of or protecting something

equity state of being treated equally

degradation act of lowering someone to a less respected state

discrimination unfair treatment based on nationality, culture, race or other personal traits

disputed doubted, called into question and disagreed upon

Dreaming First Nations peoples' understanding of the world and its creation

Elders Aboriginal and Torres Strait Islander peoples who have gained recognition as custodians of knowledge and lore, and who have permission to disclose this knowledge and beliefs

Federation Australia's coming together of states to form a federal government

indignity treatment or circumstances that cause a person to feel shame

inflicted caused suffering

legislated made law

misguided acted on with wrong information

mission area for Aboriginal and Torres Strait Islander people to live that is controlled by a Church

NAIDOC National Aborigines and Islanders Day Observance Committee

National Inquiry federally established investigations into issues of national importance

persecution unfair or cruel treatment over a long period of time, based on nationality, culture, race or other personal traits

preserved held intact for future generations to appreciate

profound very important and intense

reconciliation coming together and repairing of a relationship between two parties who have disagreed

spirituality sense of connection to something bigger than ourselves

Stolen Generations Aboriginal and Torres Strait Islander children who were wrongly taken from their families in an attempt to assimilate them into European culture

INDEX